PAIIS

#206

THE CIRCLE OF THANKS

Native American Poems and Songs of Thanksgiving

TOLD BY JOSEPH BRUCHAC

PICTURES BY MURV JACOB

BridgeWater Books

For the grandparents and the children, those whose lives are closest on the circle.   J.B.

I lovingly dedicate this book to the circle of my friends who make day to day life such a joy: Niecy, Bobby, Eddie, Garron, Drew, and Debbie, and so many others. Wa-Doh.   M.J.

A special thanks to William Douglas Bryant, for his help with this book.   M.J.

Design and art direction by Leslie Bauman.

Published by BridgeWater Books, an imprint and registered trademark of Troll Communications L.L.C.

Library of Congress
Cataloging-in-Publication Data

Bruchac, Joseph
The circle of thanks / by Joseph Bruchac; pictures by Murv Jacob.
p.   cm.
Summary: Fourteen poems with themes of thanksgiving and appreciation of nature, based in part on traditional Native American songs and prayers.
ISBN 0-8167-4012-7 (lib.)
1. Indians of North America—Juvenile poetry.
2. Gratitude—Juvenile poetry.   3. Nature—Juvenile poetry.   4. Children's poetry, American.   [1. Indians of North America—Poetry.   2. Gratitude—Poetry.
3. Nature—Poetry.   4. American poetry.]   I. Jacob, Murv, ill.   II. Title.
PS3552.R794C57   1996
811'.54—dc20   95-41175

A NOTE TO THE READER

Today, most of the people of the United States have one official day for giving thanks. That day, which we call Thanksgiving, is patterned after one of the festivals of thanksgiving, one that still occurs in the late autumn of each year, among the Wampanoag people of New England.

But, for the original Americans, one day to give thanks was not enough. There were too many things in the natural world that helped the people to survive, that made their lives fuller and better. Among the Iroquois people, a long Thanksgiving Address thanking every part of creation still opens every important gathering.

Whenever medicine plants or food plants are gathered, it is said that those plants have agreed to give themselves to the people. If they are not treated well, those plants may not continue to grow in the future. Whenever an animal gives its body to be used for food and clothing, the people express their gratitude.

Giving thanks has always helped American Indian people to appreciate and respect the lives around them. It continues to help them.

Wherever we go on this continent, we find there are many traditions of recognizing the gifts given to us. There are many ways of saying thank you. These are some of those ways.

Joseph Bruchac

THE CIRCLE OF THANKS

As I play my drum
I look around me
and I see the trees.
The trees are dancing
in a circle about me
and they are beautiful.

As I play my drum
I look around me
and I see the sun and moon.
The sun and moon are dancing
in a circle about me
and they are beautiful.

As I play my drum
I look around me
and I see the stars.
The stars are dancing
in a circle about me
and they are beautiful.

As I play my drum
I look around me
and I see my people.
All my people are dancing
in a circle about me
and my people, they are beautiful.

Micmac, Northeast Coast

THANKS TO MOTHER EARTH

Onen, we give thanks
to our mother, the Earth,
for she gives us all that we need for life.

She supports our feet
as we walk upon her.
She is there to catch us
if we should fall.

It has always been this way
since the beginning,
for she is our mother,
the one who cares for us.

It gives us great joy
that Mother Earth
continues still to care for us.

So it is that we join
our minds together
to give greetings and thanks
to this Earth, our mother.

Mohawk, Eastern Woodlands

RAIN SONG

Close to the west,
the great ocean is singing,
the waves roll toward me
covered with clouds.
Even here I catch the sound.
The earth is shaking
and I hear the deep rumbling.

A cloud is singing
on top of Evergreen Mountain,
a cloud is standing still
on top of Evergreen Mountain.
Up there it is raining,
it is raining here.
Under the mountains
the corn tassels are shaking,
under the mountains
the horns of the child corn are glistening.

Papago, Southwest

HOW MEDICINE CAME

Long ago,
the animals and the birds,
the fish and insects and plants
could all talk.
They lived with the people
in peace and friendship.

Then the people invented
bows and blowguns and spears.
They began to kill
the animals and birds and fish
for their flesh and their skins.
The animals then joined together.
They invented diseases
to weaken the people.

The plants remained friendly
to the people.
Each tree and shrub and herb agreed
to offer a cure for each new disease.
Each said, "When I am called upon,
I shall help the humans in their need."

So it is that the plants gave us medicine.
So it is that we must be thankful to them.

Cherokee, Southeast

PRAYER FOR GATHERING
CEDAR ROOTS

Look at me, my friend.
I have come to ask you
to give me some
of the fringe from your dress.

You have come to take pity on us.
There is nothing for which
you cannot be used,
because it is your way.
There is nothing
for which we cannot use you.
So it is that you are willing
to give us some of your dress.

I have come to ask you
for this, long-life maker.
I shall make a basket
from the fringe of your dress.

Kwakiutl, Northwest Coast

SONG FOR THE CORN

The mockingbird stretches his song
like ropes between the mountaintops.
The wind comes bearing the rain on its back.
And we walk together around our fields
each night, singing up the corn.

We will sing up the corn
and the corn will answer.

It will sing back to us,
blowing in the wind:

> Am I corn of two colors,
> am I crazy corn,
> singing in the wind?

> Am I corn of three colors,
> am I laughing corn,
> singing in the wind?

The corn will come up
like a feather headdress.
It will come up green,
here upon our fields.

Here upon our fields,
giving us life,
green leaves will blow in the breeze.

Papago, Southwest

THANKS TO BLACK BEAR

Thank you, friend,
that you did not make me walk about in vain.
Thank you that you allowed me to hunt you,
thank you that you allowed my arrow to strike true.

Now you have come
to take mercy on me
so that I may obtain game,
so that I may inherit your power
of getting easily the salmon you catch.

Now I press my right hand
against your left hand.

Oh, my friend,
now we press together our working hands
that you may give to me
your power of getting things easily with your hands.

Kwakiutl, Pacific Northwest

KACHINA SONG

At the edge of the cornfield
a bird will sing with them,
it will sing with them
in the oneness of happiness
and the hearts of the people
will be filled with thanksgiving.

So the people and the bird
will sing together
in tune with the universal power,
in harmony with the one Creator.

The birdsong and the people's song
and the song of life
will become one.

Hopi, Southwest

HEALING SONG OF THE WIND

The Wind now begins to sing.
The Wind now begins to sing.
The land stretches away before me,
away before me, the land stretches away.

I ask the Wind for help in healing
and the Wind begins to sing.
I thank the Wind for the help it will give
and the Wind begins to sing.

The house of Wind now is thundering.
The house of Wind now is thundering.
I go roaring over the land,
the land covered with thunder.

Over the windy mountains,
over the windy mountains
came the many-legged Wind.
The Wind came running to me.

The Black Snake Wind came to me.
The Black Snake Wind came to me.
It came and wrapped itself about me.
It came running to me with its healing songs.

Pima, Southwest

SONG FOR THUNDER

Thonah! Thonah!
There is a voice above,
the voice of thunder
within the dark cloud.
Again it sounds, again and again.
Thonah! Thonah!
Thonah! Thonah!

The voice that makes beautiful the land,
the voice above,
the voice of thunder
that brings us the rain,
within the dark cloud
it sounds again, again and again.
Thonah! Thonah!
Thonah! Thonah!

The voice that makes beautiful the land,
the voice that makes beautiful the land,
it is answered by the voice below,
the grasshopper among the plants.
Again it sounds, again and again,
the voice that makes beautiful the land.

Navajo, Southwest

PRAYER TO THE SUN

As my grandfather comes,
the one who watches all
on this earth below,
we offer him our prayers.

As his wide-spreading rays appear,
giving us the light
to see each new day,
we offer him our prayers.

As the Sun himself appears,
showing us the power
of our great Creator,
we offer him our prayers.

As his feathered shafts of light appear,
without whose warmth
life could not last,
we offer him our prayers.

As he is fully risen,
we offer him our prayers.

Osage, Great Plains

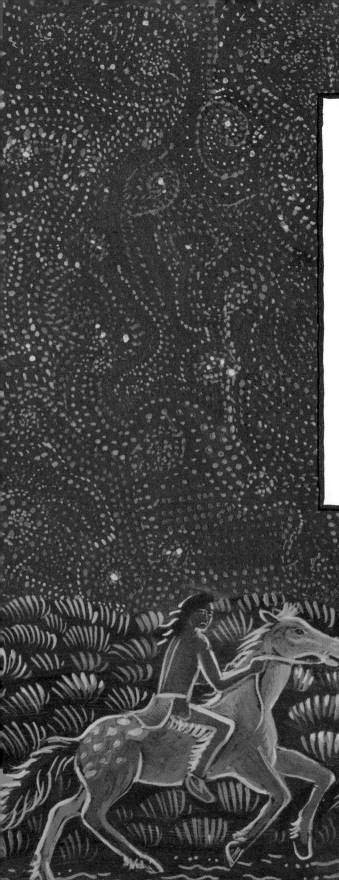

SONG TO THE DANCING STARS

Look as they rise,
look as those stars rise
there over the line
where the earth meets the sky.

Those Star Dancers,
they rise up together.
Look, as they rise up,
how they come to guide us.

They lead us safely,
they keep us as one.

Dancing Stars,
we watch you as you rise.
Teach us to be, like you, united.

Pawnee, Southern Plains

WORDS CALLED TO THE FOUR DIRECTIONS

Wakondah, the Great Mystery,
will make the coming days
to be calm and peaceful.
The Sky People and the Earth People
have called to Wakondah
to make the days calm and peaceful
so that the little ones may come to us
and pass through the four valleys of life,
through birth and youth,
through adulthood and old age.

Now Wakondah will make
the days to be beautiful
toward the winds of the rising sun.
Wakondah will make
the days to be beautiful
toward the winds of the summer lands.
Wakondah will make the days to be beautiful
toward the winds of the setting sun.
Wakondah will make
the days to be beautiful
toward the winds of the land of cedars.

Wakondah will make the days,
will make the days to be calm and peaceful.

Osage, Great Plains

AFTERWORD

So we have traveled once around the circle of thanks. We have looked at all the gifts that are around us and we have spoken words of gratitude and greeting to some of them.

Yet that circle never ends. Each time we go around it, we come back to the place where we began. And that circle belongs to each one of us. The earth and the waters, the moon and sun and stars belong to everyone.

There are many we have not thanked in these poems. Now it is your chance to think about those you would like to thank. Think about those who are part of your own circle of thanks.

NOTES

The poems in this book are based in part on traditional Native American songs and prayers. Many other Native American songs and prayers can be found in *The Indians' Book*, edited by Natalie Curtis (1923), and *The Sky Clears*, by A. Grove Day (1951).

Page 4   THE CIRCLE OF THANKS

Because the drum is round, it is a symbol of the earth, the connections between all of the people, and the fact that life itself is like a circle. Most Native dances, like those of the Micmac, are done in a big circle. When the people dance, they move in a circle like those greater circles made by the sun and moon and stars in the sky.

Page 6   THANKS TO MOTHER EARTH

Our mother gives us life and cares for us. In the same way, we get our lives and everything we need from the earth, which is called "Our Mother" in the Mohawk language. In the long Thanksgiving Prayer spoken when people come together, Mother Earth is among the first to be thanked.

Page 9   RAIN SONG

The rain is especially important to the Papago people of the dry Southwest. It comes from the west, the direction of the great ocean, and so they say that the thunder is the sound of the ocean and its loud waves. Without rain, the corn, which is one of their main foods, would not survive. The clouds are seen as living beings, which sing as it rains, while the young corn, the "child corn," dances in that life-giving rain.

Page 10   HOW MEDICINE CAME

In Cherokee belief, animals and plants are just as important as people. They live in families and can talk to each other. Medicine plants are especially important because they can be used to make such things as teas and salves to cure certain sicknesses. Many of our modern medicines, such as aspirin—which is based on a medicine found in willow bark—are from Native medicine plants. If something is given to you, you are expected to give something back in return. So the medicine plants must always be thanked for helping the people.

Page 12   PRAYER FOR GATHERING CEDAR ROOTS

The cedar tree is extremely important to the people of the northwest coast. Its wood is used for making houses and canoes, and its roots, which are long, stringy, and tough, can be easily woven into durable baskets.

Page 15   SONG FOR THE CORN

Here again, we see that the corn, that very important food plant, is viewed as a person. It dances in the wind and enjoys being sung to by the people. Wearing its green headdress, it sings back to the people. Listen to corn leaves blowing in the wind. The sound they make is like a song.

Page 16   THANKS TO BLACK BEAR

Native people often say that of all the animals, Bear is the most like a human

being. When the Kwakiutl hunt the bear, they do so because they intend to use it for food and clothing. They also believe that a man who shows the proper respect when he kills a bear will be given a special gift by the bear. He will inherit the bear's ability to catch fish and other game.

Page 19   KACHINA SONG
The kachinas of the Hopi people portray different aspects of life. At certain times of the year, these masked figures come dancing into the Hopi villages. Their dances and elaborate masks and clothing are a ceremonial way of showing people the different powers of the universe and giving thanks to them. Doll-like figures are made for Hopi children so they can learn the names and stories and songs of the many different kachinas. Many of those songs, like this one, praise specific parts of the natural world.

Page 21   HEALING SONG OF THE WIND
The Pima people know that life depends on breath. They associate the wind, which is the breath of this planet, with healing power. When a person wishes to gain some of that healing power, a song such as this one might be sung to call the wind.

Page 22   SONG FOR THUNDER
Native people often see the thunder in the form of a giant, helpful being who lives above the clouds. The Navajo welcome the rumbling voice of thunder because it means the dry season will

soon be over and the land will again grow green with the rain.

Page 25   PRAYER TO THE SUN
The sun is called Grandfather by the Osage people because of his age and his generosity. The light and warmth of the sun sustains life on the earth. The sun is viewed as one of the greatest examples of the power of the Creator, and so prayers are offered to it.

Page 27   SONG TO THE DANCING STARS
The Pleiades are a constellation of seven stars that move in a circle about the sky, in a slightly different place each night. They are seen as celestial dancers by many different Native nations. To the Pawnee of the Great Plains, they are the Star Dancers, who always remain together, faithful to each other.

Page 29   WORDS CALLED TO THE FOUR DIRECTIONS
The Osage divide themselves into two groups: the Sky People and the Earth People. Although they were the tallest of the people of the plains, they always call themselves "the little ones" because they are very small in comparison with the power of Wakondah, the Creator. Just as the earth is divided into four directions, life is divided into four valleys: birth, youth, adulthood, and old age. Spring, the direction of the rising sun, symbolizes birth, just as winter, which is from the north—"the land of the cedars"—symbolizes old age.